Michael Palma

A FORTUNE IN GOLD

Michael Palma

A FORTUNE IN GOLD

GRADIVA PUBLICATIONS ✛ STONY BROOK, NEW YORK

ISBN 1-892021-07-2

Cover photograph: Marie Eiland
Author photograph: Victoria Palma
Cover and typesetting: M^2 Design Solutions, Annandale, NJ

The author and the publisher gratefully acknowledge the generous
support of the Sonia Raiziss Giop Charitable Foundation
in the publication of this volume.

Gradiva Publications
P.O. Box 831
Stony Brook, NY 11790

Thanks are due to the editors of the following journals, in whose pages some of the poems in this collection originally appeared:

Café Review: "By the Old Canal," "In Time," "Lines," "The Patron Saint of California"; *The Cornelian:* "Christ in the Cradle"; *Edge City Review:* "After Thoreau," "Nothing to Get Hung About"; *Italian Americana:* "Let Me Take You Down," "Read Carefully Before Using"; *Northeast:* "All the Conquerors" 3, "Cats," "The Flowers," "In the Afternoon," "In the End," "Talk," "Two by Two"; *Pivot:* "An Evening Out," "Ray Charles at the Copa," "Song," "Year of Our Grace."

"Cats" was reprinted in *Remember That Symphonies Also Take Place in Snails,* edited by John and Joanne Judson (Juniper Press, 1989).

For TOM PENDLETON,
who taught me much about poetry
and more about humanity.

CONTENTS

3

The world won't be the same without Big Daddy.
Or else it will be.

Randall Jarrell

I always think there's a band, kid.

Prof. Harold Hill

.

1

An Evening Out

The longed-for night is here at last.
The tickets posted months before
Are handed over at the door,
And we proceed to wriggle past
A spread of seven hundred souls
Filling a bright and massive hall.
Houselights and conversations fall.
A liquid piano line unrolls,
Met by a stab of violins.
Some press their fingertips and stare,
Some bow their heads as if in prayer.
And very soon my mind begins
To slide, my thoughts begin to run
Down thorny paths and twisting slopes—
Today's mistakes, tomorrow's hopes,
The could have been and should have done,
The wasted and the waiting years—
Until my consciousness loops round
To fix once more upon the sound
That breaks and shimmers in my ears.
I start to listen, passionately
Awaiting when it will have passed
So that I may begin at last
To savor it in memory.

Ray Charles at the Copa

He stands in shadow, waiting to go on,
Alone inside his mind as mother care
Sits aching in his muscles. Spotlights flare,
The trumpets call his name, his frown is gone.

He hovers at the piano, reaches out
And like a woman it is one with him,
Rippling in his rhythms. Spotlights dim.
He hunches down into his edging shout.

He strains for every wound on every skin
Until they open out along his flesh,
Ripe and sparkling. The ripped pieces mesh
Into a mouth that sucks the darkness in.

He moans and rocks, the piano rocks and screams,
Soul flares its fingers and the body dreams.

Dancing as May Be Credible

(Twyla Tharp: "Deuce Coupe")

Slide wiggle trip across the floor,
The floor is all you have
To sustain you.

Offer a hip to the air,
Flip and revolve.
Rain in your fingertips is the only rain.

Cry form, cry measure
Where the only measure's
The distance you disjoint.

Resolve a flat world with a rolling shoulder,
Dip and strut and shuffle,
Point resistance

With your splayed self
With your glib neck
With your breath.

Peck with your nose at enlightened sky,
It will deny you nothing.

Cats

They hear you coming
Before you know you're coming.
They suck up wisdom
From your eyes.

Their eyes turn colors
In the turning light.
They frown like owls.
They yawn

And then the fangs.
The light that holds the tiny dust,
The falling leaves,
The falling snow,

They live in a city of toys.
Claws ripple underneath the fur,
They sit up with dead spiders.
Fluent machines, they balance

Existence on the tips
Of their noses.
They love themselves
With your hand.

Pig

Pig in his gravity walks
Over the wholesome earth
Dressed in himself.
He utters his weather.

Aurelian trees
Assured and emblematic
Define his setting.
Outposts are established.

Chickens have no being.
Horses have no being.
Pig the faithful beast
Squanders his ripe aromas.

He grunts and roots
In his tight little shoes,
A gasping heart
Among the crumbling leaves.

The Flowers

Who wants to hear
All about the flowers,
All the splendid shoots,
The delicate names?
How they take no thought
For the heart's desire—
So perishable,
So lightly arrayed?

Who wants to know
How they put to shame
All our solid rubbish,
Our heavy dreams?
How they lean toward heaven
And live in air?
Who loves the flowers
Will never love me.

Almanac

Winter is final,
Stopping the sun in the middle of his road,
Drying the roads to a brittle consistency.
Here in the land
Where all the seasons come,
The pages stand long enough to be read.
The skies contend
As we contend with one another,
The wind blows through the letters of our names.
Trees are smaller, filigreed.
We sit in still houses listening to the wind,
To little bones inside us
That crackle in the night.

Spring is familiar,
Every leaf placed in yesterday's landscape.
In our rememberings, it's always spring.
Light jackets, sunlight adhering
To the glazed walls of shops,
To the gelatin trees.
Numbers pass by,
Bright with colors, tinkling with little bells.
Sweetness catches halfway down.
We reach for the numbers,
And as they bounce away we have to laugh.
We reach for the sweetness.
Nothing can be touched.

Summer is fever,
Wide days pressing on our foreheads
When things can happen impossible in snow.
Lines crawl across the moon,
Making small patterns.
Night twitches on rustling porches.
We confess our love for women
Whose faces we can't recall.
A piano plays, delicate and far,
Each note hooked lightly to the one before.
Eyes closed, we see the tiny hooks,
The notes dropping into place,
Till sun returns, flooding the passages.

Autumn is faithful,
Curving the roads again,
Turning the houses wooden and brown.
Water gurgles over rocks,
Leaves dance between our feet.
Now we like to sit
In the afternoon with those we love.
We have given our lives away without a thought.
Brass coins hang from the trees,
The branches bend with their weight
Low enough to be plucked.
At night men tread their shadows,
Coins in their pockets, leaning to one side.

Winter is finest.
In virgin winter we fondle perfect dreams
Of recollected spring.
Green lives in the mind,
Brighter and sharper than day can afford.
The clocks turn slowly as we clear the glass.
With windows bared on every side
The weather clamps about us,
Lining the land in crisp geometry.
As suddenly as the silence overhead
The horizons reconfigure.
Now we walk the land
Straightforwardly, into the weather.

Lines

The wide creation
Leans toward the moment,
Lines of necessity
Converge.

The engine approaches,
Shakes the trestle,
Crosses
To the other side.

The farmers
Watch the train go past,
They watch the wheels
Go round and round.

Philosopher's Stone

If I can't have love
I can still have me,
One bite at a time
Will satisfy.

The air is yellow,
The insides too.
What's it to me
With my pot of paint?

With six words
I can make a world,
With two hands
I can gather me.

The dirt gets into
My little holes.
How else do I know
That I'm still here?

If I can't be happy
I can be filthy,
Kiss the world
And call it me.

Let Me Take You Down

(Home for disturbed children)

Turn out your eyes but never see,
Don't ever lock the door on me,
You've got enough hot privacy
Up in your head where I can't be.
Stay in there, it's deep and black.
One step forward, one step back.

I'll pull you out of bed at eight,
Put bars across the garden gate.
Get your shoes on, don't be late.
Ready? Now sit there and wait.
Put my garbage in your sack.
Two steps forward, two steps back.

Come out come out, but never play,
Snatch a quick spoonful of day.
Passers stare but never say,
Get their fill and look away.
Hop home across the railroad track,
Three steps forward, three steps back.

Hide inside your bed all night,
Watch out for the hungry light.
Keep your tiny world locked tight,
Never find out which one's right.
Take it all, you can't attack.
One step forward, one step back.

Nothing to Get Hung About

He was wrong, he knew it, he was the teacher, he
Had to back his shredded argument. The child,
Lost in his rightness, publicly stupid, smiled
To no one, "I don't know what's wrong with me,
I guess I just don't want to be any more."
His file said genius. He was just turned four.

"Is that what they call you?" And the doctor said
A stabbing word that children just turned five
Don't say, in books. The boy's laugh was a shout—
"I always make a mess of things!"—already
Wearing his bull's-eye. Please keep me alive,
His eyes were saying, don't let me fall out.

They kept him alive to weather, alive to night,
To what boiled up inside him, not much more.
Time went, so he went with it, just as far
As it would take him, just to see what might
Be waiting for him, trying now and then
His dances on the edge, but hanging in.

Read Carefully Before Using

Respect the setters of standards, the justifiers,
Whose reasons are the same as their desires.
Esteem the droves who are doing as they should,
Who look upon their works and find them good.
Value the ones whose consciences uphold them,
Whose fluffed, upholstered memories enfold them.
Honor the hosts who can't help how they feel:
Thought is no substitute for honest zeal.

Admire the plump and sleek who are warm with knowing
That hell awaits the wicked, whose list is growing.
Cherish the cherubs who cheerfully admit
They are here for a reason, and know the reason too.
Envy the swarms who can't smell their own shit:
There's a whole lot more of it than there is of you.

With Boughs of Holly

I mind me one Christmas out in the country,
We had no tree. It was twenty below that year,
No money, a war on too. Oh, we just hated
To disappoint the kids of course, but what could we do?
My husband's father was living with us then.
He used to say, "I've had me the very best treatment
This place has got to give me, and here I am
Still dying. All them doctors, all them failures.
Ha!" Then, just three days shy of Christmas
He up and died on us. Well sir, we waited a bit
As we thought was proper, then stood him right up
In a big old pot we kept in the shed
And never could find the use of, painted his face green,
Stuck out his arms kind of crosslike, stuck in
Some little branches here and there,
Ornaments, tinsel and such, had us a fine handsome tree.
All in all, God's taken care of us, I'd say.

The Patron Saint of California

The patron saint of California
Wears both of his eyes
On one side of his face.
His head is long and curved,
Tilted to one side.
His nose points inward.
His face is turned
Westward, toward
The vast and cloudless sea.

He stands at the summit
Of a plump mountain
And whispers to the valley.
When the townsmen hear
His low, harsh croon
They put down their cabbages
And walk together, arms
Linked, laughing
And singing, down to the sea.

Christ in the Cradle

Christ in the cradle
  Shielded from sin,
Flesh round a godhead
  Uncoiling within,
An absolute voice
  Whose iron commands
Waited to master
  Your innocent hands.
Babe born of woman,
  Heart opened wide,
Mind with no corner
  Where you could hide.

Counting My Corpses

It's easier than was thought. The body crunched
Under the tires, the drivers' voices skirling,
Kibitzers on the sidewalks taking sides,
The red lights flashing, the disgusted cops.

The red lights flashing all along the chest,
Throat choking back the thick sweet blood, the spoon
Bouncing away from the table, the face falling into
The hot tomato soup, the stains on the wall.

The hot tomato soup curdling the insides,
The jerking away in a dry ratchety cough,
The spongy alveoli thick and thicker,
The thin lines pounding up and down the arms.

The thin lines pounding, bursting behind the eyes,
The eager platelets spotting the weary brain,
Cells cutting loose in twisted efflorescence,
One of the million madly multiplying.

One of the million things that could have happened
Becomes the only thing that could have happened,
Establishing nothing, hardening everywhere,
Patches of gray collecting into black.

Patches of gray collecting on the knuckles,
Smutchings from inside out, the bone joints cracking
In the littlest doing, all the ribs contracting,
Popping the heart right out of the mouth.

Popping the heart pushes the brain to spasm,
Stumbling toward the door, where is the door
That gives on the endlessness of mathematics?
The ripe flesh pimpling in the understanding.

The ripe flesh pimpling in the lightest breezes
Gathers to parchment, the nimbus in the eyes
Dims like an ancient bulb, the rounded mouth
Sinks back forever in the hungry vacuum.

Sinks back behind immaculate machines
Rinse out the organs. They go into bottles,
Float in the middle, where nothing can befall them.
It's easier to believe than to recall them.

In Time

A fox stops
In western Pennsylvania
In the middle of a field.

An old man in a boardinghouse
Talks softly to himself
As he eats his soup.

Snow is falling
All over Pennsylvania,
The air is moving.

A woman on a bus
Reads in the newspaper
About other people's troubles.

The paper is two days old.
The soup is good and hot.
The fox moves on.

2

Women

Women have sharp things to say about us.
Which of us can tell what is on their minds?

Their blue visions bejewel the ceiling,
Their swift occasions swell the glad noon.

Men, the slow primates with hair on themselves:
Touch the black hair, touch the yellow hair.

Women's green poems with dark soil below,
They have more meanings than we can use.

When women hurt they slash the red nerves,
The birds hide their faces in simple fear.

Roundelay

"Would you like to come in?" he asked,
And she looked at him as if
No woman had ever entered his house
For a decent purpose. He smiled.

"What do you think about?" she asked,
Trailing her fingers along the table,
Turning from the waist.
He stepped behind her. "Oh,

About a woman coming here,
Bringing me her personal body,
Me showing her its separate life,
Giving her toes new reasons to exist."

He sipped at her ear. "About the tawny
Nape that hides beneath her hair."
His fingers tiptoed up her ribs
To find the doorbells of desire.

"Give up your fantasy to me,
Let me make it true for you."
The bed was moving across the room,
Coming to meet them. He turned her around.

Now he was doing strong things with her
Now he was open and upon her
Rushing sliding tumbling to her
As far as his mind could take her

Now she was climbing to meet him
Their bodies moaned together
Their minds flew out the window
They came apart everywhere

Loosely fastened, brains seeping back,
They lay. Cradling him,
She wondered who he was.
"What do you think about?" he asked.

Two by Two

He tortured her down to the bone, and still
He scraped again, until she found his side.
He danced allegros all across her will,
For there were more important things than pride.

She tortured him and basted through his brain
And rioted within with rack and whip
Until he heard his mind begin to drip,
For there were more important things than pain.

He tortured her until the marrow bled.
He held his eyes to keep them in his head.
He licked her lips. She bent to kiss the knife.
For there were more important things than life.

Not with a Bang

Samuel was much possessed by flesh
And saw the breast beneath the brace.
His contemplations tumbled free,
His bursting pen scratched on apace.

Creative fires lit the room
And made his nightpiece stand on end
To spawn his nubile heroine
(Envy, be silent and attend).

Pamela was of an upright stamp
(O hymen and O hymenee),
No tickling trollop she, to stoop
To sixpence sensuality.

Her comforter in the long night
Was Virtue, standing just beyond
Until it was proposed to by
A five percent exchequer bond.

Wheels of Spring

With his hard feet,
With his straight arms,
With his multichambered
Heart, he says no
He says no, he says
Hell with them all,
Let them go,
Let them go. He turns
On his other side.
The alarm says hello.
Bicycles dance
On the round horizon,
The leaves are birds,
The spring rains
Have overflowed
His stream again.
He doesn't believe
In any of it,
He says yes,
He says yes, as
A bottle of milk
Dances over the table.
He says well,
He says now,
With his quick hands,
With his quick cells,

With the multidimensional
Eyes in his head.

2

Swarmflies buzzing
In the light,
Screenflies breeding
On the yellow porch.
Curtains rippling,
Eyes scanning night,
And the night says
He is coming.
The flies hide
As he comes to her.
They cling and kiss.
The flies regroup.
Her silver tongues
Assail him now,
They scream within
Triumphantly. The flies
Attach themselves
To the screen.
Who will love him
As she loves him,
Who'll hold him
In the throat of night?

No one, no one
In the long world.
On the porch
The flies lie dead
Of ecstasy,
With embarrassed faces.

3

Spring is come again,
The season when
He wonders who
Would be better off
Without him. Himself
He puts somewhere
In the middle
Of the list.
Believer in love,
He waits for her
To imagine him.
Believer in love,
He has as much
As the one who believes
In nothing. Nothing
Is all his study.
If he had a stick
He would beat himself.

But he has no stick.
If he had a knife
He would slit his throat.
But he has no knife.
If he had hands
He would claw his eyes.
But he has hands.
He looks at them,
He looks at them.
He looks at them.

Not All the Blood of Goats

"Not all the blood of goats
Shall for my sins atone..."

He followed after women as
It's done by one who feels he has
Been nudged by some great master plan
That plumps the destiny of man.
He was the kind that fell in love
Piecemeal: he lay dreaming of
One woman's smile, another's eyes,
Another's arabesques and sighs,
Another's legs, another's song
Whose melody had made him long.
But being sensible he knew
This sort of thing would never do.
He put a hood upon his head.
He spoke as little as the dead.
He fingered beads excitedly.
He nailed desire to a tree.
He ate black bread and stinking stew.
But two red eyes were eating too.
In the light they were Christ-size.
In the night they were the eyes
Of a woman who with toes uncurled
Had kissed him halfway round the world.
And being sensible he knew
This sort of thing would never do.
He ran to gatherings of wise

Young men with irritated eyes
Who closed their circles with a twist
That told him he would not be missed.
He ran to gatherings of old
Disgruntled men who sat and told
How they had been respected once,
And wiped their hands on their shirtfronts.
They drove him out again with stares
That said his sorrows cheapened theirs.
He walked into the crowded street
And offered to wash any feet
That needed washing or did not,
And begged the chance to kiss the blot
Of any human who believed.
But scorn was all that he received.
He strayed into the thoroughfare
Where traffic was its thickest, where
He threatened God he would stand still
Upon that very spot until
He heard God whisper in his ear,
And consequently did not hear
The truck that knocked him neatly flat.
He lay a while, and then he sat,
Stood up, shook hands, then said good day
And smiled contritely, walked away,
Head mercifully cleansed of sense,
And never knew the difference.

The Grateful Heart

He felt the blood rush from the bud
    And waited to be plucked.
She happened there, she sniffed the air.
    They looked, and he was tucked.

She made him high, she made him dry,
    She sealed him in a box
To keep him snug while she cut a rug.
    He polished up the locks.

She gave a taste, then laid him waste.
    Perhaps he had been asking?
Warmed by the fire of his desire,
    She stoked, and kept on basking.

She left him shorn, but unreborn.
    He wept and hoped and hid.
When would he find another one
To care for him as she had done?
    With luck, he never did.

By the Old Canal

If only there were music
    We could dance.

Awash in amniotic data,
    Anomie and blague,
All the old words
    Cascading in a mantra,
Until quietly he told her,
    Ours is a perfect romance.
You are always possible,
    A check I'll never cash.
Distant, unrealizable,
    Yet comforting—a star.
To say more would be madness.
    We must never meet again.

If only we could dance
    There would be music.

Notes from a Dry Place

1

I (you, he) buy the papers
At the corner every morning.
I buy the magazines every week,
The ones with the brighter covers.

I never read them.
I'm always too busy
Moving the dust and putting it back,
Moving the blood and putting it back.

2

For the first time in our time
No war distracts us.
Unready for victory,
New flags fly, old flags fly.

Shooting is private
And meaningful. Diplomats pose
For photographs, grinning:
Now what happens?

3

If you would read the poems,
My (his, your) poems,
I know you would like them.
If you would listen to me

I would make you happy.
If I would be happy.
If the sun would come up,
If the sun would go down.

4

I buy records now,
Going from store to store,
Mumbling, bothering the clerks,
Till I find the ones I want.

I play them once
And then forget about them.
I thought I couldn't live without them
And I was right.

5

Sky comes over gray,
Long shadows come over the houses.
No rain now for two weeks.
Rain, that would be something.

You would be in a house,
I would be in a house, not watching
What passes with you (him, us)
For happiness these days.

6

Now things begin to happen
That I was told about.
Hair falls, feet fall,
Teeth crumble in my head.

The faces of my dead
Dissolve, the names refuse themselves.
All the colors brown. Who knew
That this would happen?

7

Nothing matters, nothing goes away.
Clutter assembles.
The roofs take on a steeper angle,
The sparrows hold on tighter.

If I could do what I want
I think I'd wait.
I get up and walk
Into the lamplight of a bright emptiness.

8

Are the poems nice?
They don't want to be nice.
They want to be raw and sneaky
And wait for you in dark corners.

They want to thrum with your secrets
And get you where it hurts.
I mean well, I suppose,
But they don't.

9

The smile that lives with you,
Your eyes that know and know,
Your definite nose.
I carry them.

You have another face
In the daylight, other hands.
You watch me out of eyes
From another face.

10

Too much time listening to myself,
Too many little habits.
No one to tell me what an ass I am,
To hold up a different frame.

I don't want words,
I don't want pictures for another time.
Words don't get me the things I want,
Not any of them.

11

If the dust would move
From one place to another,
If the blood would move
From one place to another,

I could walk like any other jackass
In the street, saying hello.
If I could hate him (them, me)
I could be happy.

12

The sun will come up,
The sun will go down.
There will be new papers in the morning
And new wars.

There will be new magazines,
More frightened faces,
New records, always something
To keep us going.

Talk

Snugly as if
In the middle of
A dark wood
They formed
Together on
The bed

(Beyond the door
The heads talked
And the hands
Talked and the
Talking faces
Talked)

Hands moved
Hesitating
In the stillness
Where they met
All that waited
And approved

(Out beyond
They talked and
Talked around
Ezra Pound God
Honor country and
All that and)

Then with
Smooth strokes
She moved him:
Ah!
(But you must
Understand

Before we can
Have true
Communication
We must first
Define our)
Ah!

Song

Not the prettiness all packaged
But the craftsmanship sustains,
Independence nicely managed
From the bottom through the brains.

Not the once forever jottings
Splashed on suicidal air.
In a spangled doublet starting
End in tattered underwear.

Not mush apples turning mellow,
Singing down they dance to sleep.
Where the cock crows heart will pillow,
When the cock falls heart will keep.

I Wanted to Write

I wanted to write
A poem for you,
A poem to say
I love you.

It wouldn't come.
Finally I said
I'd say it this way:
I love you,

And for once
Be understood
By those who know
Nothing about art.

In the Afternoon

A woman, heavy-thighed,
Spreads darkness to the day,
To him. He slips inside
And slips away
From everything that lurks
In absolute disguise,
From all eternal works.
When they arise,
He chastened and uncurled,
She thoughtful, they are freed
To choose from all this world,
Choose what they need.

3

Give Us This Day

Another blonde is hacked to bits,
Another peace talk goes to hell.

In letters indignation throbs,
In op-ed columns pundits warn.

One page of three-named wealthy brides:
One has a chubby, pleasant face.

Some creeps give Orphan Annie fits,
Some crooks have Tracy down a well.

Now stars align: Avoid new jobs,
Now love lies waiting to be born.

And on the back page someone slides
Forever into second base.

The Tower

A hermit's air combines,
Dust filters down all over.
Shelves sag under unread books,
No radio
No television plays,
Though records sometimes.
Hermits like to sing.

The Czar of all the Russias
Sits in the gutter
Watching the snow turn bright red
Where his legs should be.
Imperial troops
Clatter across the square
Shooting down everyone in sight.

A hermit knows nothing
Of any of this,
Moving his books from here to there,
Pulling his fingers cha cha cha,
Running his little machines,
Constructing a world
Comfortable like smelly clothes.

Assassins keep notebooks now,
Shooting blame in all directions:
"They wouldn't let me hump my frog,"
Blowing kisses to reporters.
The prosecution jumps up sweating,

"Your Honor, I object!"
Who doesn't?

A hermit traces his window frame,
The sagging world
Turns once again,
Druids gather in the forest
Chanting the funeral of time.
Night holds. The house holds night.
Sweet dust is coming down.

All the Conquerors

I would know my shadow and my light,
so shall I at last be whole.
        Michael Tippett, *A Child of Our Time*

1

Columns of short-haired Romans
Flatten out the roadway.
The faithful in the tunnel
Twitch under a common shawl.

Lev Nikolayevich pokes in the garden,
His beard matted with greatness.
He stares at his admirers.
"I don't understand you at all."

The prizewinner in the caftan
Writes in his empty farmhouse.
Inoffensive snow is dropping
In the deep ruts of the wheel.

Adolf Hitler's favorite poet
Broods atop the painted mountain.
Ironworks in the valley
Stunt the clean limbs of the soul.

Long congresses assemble
In the polished mausoleums.
In the panels of museums
Geometric Jordans roll.

2

The steelgrey thirties. The London skies were dark.
He turned his face against the grinning ghosts,
Mummy breath drifting from the conference windows.

Sweating fish still steamed on corner carts.
He looked in crooked lanes for strictness of heart.
Nobody thought the world would ever be different.

Spain gathered him. Black thunder opened him.
He lay in the leavened dust twisted like rope
And the smirking ravens ate up all his poems.

3

A little Hitler lives in every heart
Like any Christ. He has his standard size.
In little hearts he takes the lion's part
And starts to roar, to nobody's surprise.

In larger hearts, the ones that have balloons,
The Hitler hides behind the cellar stairs.
Sometimes he growls and sings his dirty tunes
And kicks the wall, and no one ever cares.

And sometimes in September they all fight.
The cave hearts push the others to the wall,
The mansion hearts shake hands and say We're right,
Fill their balloons with bombs and let them fall.

And when it's over, all the cleancut men
Bury the bodies and say Never again.

4

Hitler was a little baby
Sitting on his daddy's knee
And his daddy was the biggest bristling man
In all the whole country
As far as he could see.

Then Hitler was a soldier
Squinting under a tree
And he heard the screams and he saw the shells
And he dreamed how real it could be
To bleed for Germany.

Now Hitler was ascending
He stood on the balcony
And he saw all the people waiting below
For a man of destiny
To tell them how to be.

So Hitler told the people
How real it all could be
If they put their souls in his iron heart
And bled to make him free
So they made it history.

O Hitler smashed the images
And he hammered sweet Jesus to a tree
But the blood squirted into Hitler's eyes
Until he couldn't see
And his own nails set him free.

5

Slabs of desire
Roar in the forests
Gods of the innards
Ferret the sun

Fences uprooted
Forests expanding
Straitness and shape
Undone undone

6

The movies hone the memories,
The bomber jackets, the white scarves,
The cigarettes, the crinkly smiles,
The crumpled girlfriends,
The stiff-shouldered wives.

Called from desks, fields, factories,
Pulled from their only lives,
Stripped, calibrated, filled, and hurled,
They gave themselves away
To save the world.

7

It was afternoon,
And now it is evening.
It is almost time
To begin a new life.
The Russians will come,
Then the Americans.

Alone in the corner,
The servants crouch.
Nobody speaks.
When the servants saw
Everyone smoking,
They knew he was dead.

8

Thousand-year-old walls lie in the street.
Arms and faces lie beneath the walls.
Impassive birds dip low above the river.

Nine-year-olds swipe butts. Their blistered feet
Patter across the bodies. Stillness falls.
The walls are sucked into the cold forever.

The beasts are dead, the master race is run.
The self-survivors trudge home wearily
Across the places they have blown away.

Semblances reassemble. Everyone
Wants to go to America, where life is free,
Where history starts over every day.

The shivering conquerors never question why
The devil's trumpet blew them from their beds
And dropped them to stand guard in the wolf's traces.

Deep in the vaults the grainy newsreels lie,
Numbered and filed by those who leave their treads
Along a roadway paved with arms and faces.

9

Having his one chance to be human,
The son of heaven came to the microphone.

Across the bright paper islands
They heard his voice.

Generals opened themselves
In the smoldering courtyards.

He slipped back behind the wall,
Having had his one chance to be real.

10

In the photograph
Is sunlight sunlight everywhere
On open throats and on our hair.
We grin and laugh.

Where the devil fell
The ancient monsters are asleep.
We squat for all time on a jeep.
We are as blond as hell.

King

The night before, he told them
It was all right now,
Death didn't make a difference.
No magic, only a knowing,
A trust in the bones.

On the balcony
In the middle of a sentence,
"You know...,"
Just as if everyone
Always knew

—And then
The air cracked down the middle,
His body sprawled
As bodies don't sprawl
When men are still inside.

No need to be old and tired,
Freighted with virtue,
Turning to wood.
The reach for the possible died
On the balcony, the absolute began.

October 1968

Leaves fall from trees, obeying older laws.
A brilliant bowl of sunlight ruminates.
In Minnesota musing sits and waits
The totem we pushed forward in our cause.
The others still weave garlands from the straws.
One shows his crimson neck and freely hates.
The oily favorite booms through ghost debates
With sweating straw men, managing applause.
The other one recirculates the saws
Of humanness, and prays the bully fates
Won't pull apart his building blocks of states.
We follow this one, but with swollen craws.

The nights turn breezy, chillier. The smell
Of coming ice drifts inland from the bay
Where splintered yachts begin to slip away.
I walk outside in shirtsleeves, and I dwell
On choice of prisons. Wear the leper's bell
Around my neck, or kiss the martyr's gray?
Showing his wounds in Oregon today,
My candidate could see me in my cell
But won't unlock it for me. What the hell
Did I expect? What did I want to say?
Our gates aren't pearly, and our angels pray
For bully pleasures and beg us not to tell.

After Thoreau

The mass of men lead lives
Of quiet desperation.
For every one who strives
When misery arrives,
Ten shrivel in frustration.

The blood proposes riot.
For each one pricked to try it,
Scores mutter, and let pass.
More desperately quiet
Grow the lives that men amass.

All indications show where
All pathways bring them nowhere.
Too schooled to suffer needs,
How quietly men go where
Their desperation leads.

Three Ballads

1

They found him in the alley
They took him to the jail
They kicked him in the belly
And said there'd be no bail.

Monster! said the sergeant
Monster! said the chief
Monster! said the man
Who had no truck with grief.

Kill him! said the sergeant
Kill him! said the chief
Kill him! said the man
Who had helped his unbelief.

They took him to the courthouse
They stood him in the dock
They talked for twenty minutes
By the courthouse clock.

Guilty! said the jury
Guilty! said the judge
Guilty! said the man
Who said he bore no grudge.

Death! said the jury
Death! said the judge
Death! said the man
Whose conscience had no smudge.

They tied his hands behind him
They stood him to the wall
They fired their long rifles
And watched his body fall.

Hooray! said the left wing
Hooray! said the right
Hooray! said the man
Who was not too proud to fight.

Thank God! said the left wing
Thank God! said the right
Trading honest tears together
In the uncomplaining light.

2

"Evil, fear evil!"
    The presbyters cried.
"The presence of evil
    Cannot be denied.

The heart of the beast
    Is corrupt at the core.
The brain schemes its booty,
    What else is it for?

The chain of the cancer
    Continues to grow,
And evil's the answer.
    That's all we need know."

"That's just what we need
    To forget," he replied.
"Those notions belong
    To the days when men died

To bring back the sun.
    We should know better now.
We must look to the mind
    To understand how

With the traumas inside them
    Defenses grow thick.
We must cherish and guide them,
    Not punish the sick."

One night, as he stopped
      When the light had turned red,
Two thugs set upon him
      And left him for dead.

His comforters came
      To the ward where he bled
With wires and tubes
      Running out of his head.

They prayed and paraded
      In shifts round his bed:
"Now are you persuaded?"
      "Well...maybe," he said.

3

All the sadeyed socialists
Whose souls renounce the sake of art
Embrace the program that enlists
The simple goodness of the heart.

In shoebox towns across the land
Ten thousand mills and factories
Eroding now on every hand
Enclose their upright reveries.

As winter shadows congregate
Into their decent homes they come
To sit in dignity and wait
The trumpet of millennium.

All the sadeyed socialists
Go on their picnics in the spring
Where all the meadow's amethysts
And pearls surround them as they sing.

Their ancient melodies still lilt
Of Mooney in the endless hole
Of Joe Hill on the cross of gilt
And Debs of the unguarded soul.

They set up barricades of will
Where no one's soldiers ever come
And hoard their spiritual bill
Against the true millennium.

All the sadeyed socialists
Submit their visions in the fall
Trying to slice away the cysts
That hold our fertile hearts in thrall.

Revealed in their own dialect
With the precision of a rhyme
Their propositions still connect
And reconnect out of all time.

Marching until our hearts are free
Knowing the glory days will come
They close their eyes at night to see
The fields of the millennium.

Opportunity to Squeal

The word was given out that season
That the existence of God had been established,
The proof lying in the absence
Of any link between getting and deserving.
On hearing this, many humble folk
Were seen to dance and clap their hands,
While others beat their heads upon the pavement.
Meanwhile, the richest gnof in town
Paused a moment in the lighting of a cigar,
As if he had looked out his office window
And noticed the sun suddenly
Shining in the middle of a thunderstorm.

The word having circulated that the padre
Had concealed a fortune in gold,
The bandits forced their way into his cabin
And demanded its surrender.
They knew of course that the treasure
Was only the great faith he had instilled
In the hearts of the humble folk,
But having come this far they felt compelled
To see the situation through.
Imagine their consternation upon finding,
While prying up the floorboards
In order to hide his body, a fortune in gold.

Year of Our Grace

By cable and through hazy air,
Bosoms and chainsaws are broadcast.
We settle in a spongy chair,
Headpieces filled with straw at last.

Boiled eggs lie capsized in the pan
Of water from the morning meal.
On details skims the life of man,
Who dislocates his balance wheel.

Inflated girls attend in throes
As padded hulks bestrew the grid.
Water and kudos wait for those
Who rise to plunge as they are bid.

Ventriloquists of Jesus rap.
Confessionals sans booth and door
Carry the inside out. We nap
To rumblings of a distant war.

The Midnight Clear

Christmas comes down all over the world.
Over the rim of the world
You can see them coming,
Marching, marching, the stolid Russians.

Driving all night through the well-loved land,
Whistling softly past the quilted fields,
We will not fail
The promise and the star.

Shape without form, gesture without motion—
Who believes that any more?
Christmas is in the air.
We think of our loved ones all safe in their beds.

The Russians are waiting at the border, eating
The last of what they brought with them.
They bring messages and gifts
From the folks back home.

We turn our collars down and pray,
Let everyone be happy this one time.
The candles are in bloom, and love is coming down.
Let it shine one time for me.

In the End

Poetry won't save us in the end,
Love won't save us
And not Jesus. In the end

We will die and be translated.
Everything says itself
Without meaning to.

Let the sentences walk out
In their new suits.
Who knows what anyone may imagine?

We peel the layers of the self
And stop just in time
In a Chinese light, penetrating and cool.

Michael Palma is the author of two chapbooks of poetry, *The Egg Shape* and *Antibodies*. He has published translations of several Italian poets: Guido Gozzano (*The Man I Pretend to Be*), Diego Valeri (*My Name on the Wind*), Sergio Corazzini (*Sunday Evening*), Armando Patti (*The Eye Inside the Wind*), and Luigi Fontanella (*The Transparent Life and Other Poems*).

With Dana Gioia, he co-edited *New Italian Poets;* with Alfredo de Palchi, he co-edited *The Metaphysical Streetcar Conductor: Sixty Poems of Luciano Erba*. He has published translations of more than 150 Italian poems in journals, including *Paris Review, Grand Street,* and *Poetry,* and anthologies, including *Dialect Poetry of Southern Italy*, *Dialect Poetry of Northern Italy,* and *Via Terra,* all edited by Luigi Bonaffini.

Forthcoming volumes of his translations include books by Franco Buffoni, Paolo Valesio, and other poets, with Gradiva; *The Siege,* a sequence by the young poet Ljuba Merlina Bortolani, with BOA Editions: and Dante's *Inferno,* with W. W. Norton & Co.

His essays, reviews, and other prose pieces have appeared in *Chelsea, Shakespeare Newsletter, Italian Americana, Boston Book Review,* and *The Oxford Companion to Twentieth Century Poetry in English*. He assisted Ernest Menze in the translation of two volumes of the writings of Johann Gottfried Herder, *Selected Early Works 1764-1767* and *On World History*.

He lives in New Rochelle, New York.